Nn

Kelly Doudna

Published by SandCastle™, an imprint of ABDO Publishing Company, 4940 Viking Drive, Edina, Minnesota 55435.

Printed in the United States.

Cover and interior photo credits: Comstock, Digital Stock, Eyewire, PhotoDisc, Stockbyte

Library of Congress Cataloging-in-Publication Data

Doudna, Kelly, 1963-
    Nn / Kelly Doudna.
       p. cm. -- (The alphabet)
    ISBN 1-57765-434-X
      1. Readers (Primary) [1. Readers] I. Title.

PE1119 .D683 2001
428.1--dc21

00-056896

The SandCastle concept, content, and reading method have been reviewed and approved by a national advisory board including literacy specialists, librarians, elementary school teachers, early childhood education professionals, and parents.

Let Us Know

After reading the book, SandCastle would like you to tell us your stories about reading. What is your favorite page? Was there something hard that you needed help with? Share the ups and downs of learning to read. We want to hear from you! To get posted on the ABDO Publishing Company Web site, send us email at:

sandcastle@abdopub.com

About SandCastle™
Nonfiction books for the beginning reader

- Basic concepts of phonics are incorporated with integrated language methods of reading instruction. Most words are short, and phrases, letter sounds, and word sounds are repeated.

- Readability is determined by the number of words in each sentence, the number of characters in each word, and word lists based on curriculum frameworks.

- Full-color photography reinforces word meanings and concepts.

- "Words I Can Read" list at the end of each book teaches basic elements of grammar, helps the reader recognize the words in the text, and builds vocabulary.

- Reading levels are indicated by the number of flags on the castle.

Look for more SandCastle books in these three reading levels:

Level 1 (one flag)	**Level 2** (two flags)	**Level 3** (three flags)

Grades Pre-K to K 5 or fewer words per page	**Grades K to 1** 5 to 10 words per page	**Grades 1 to 2** 10 to 15 words per page

Nora and Ned have fun.

Norm needs a net.

Nolan stands near
a tire.

Nola lies on the lawn.

Nate has an inner tube.

Nat has a neat
horse.

Nick holds a kitten.

Nicki is nice to Nami.

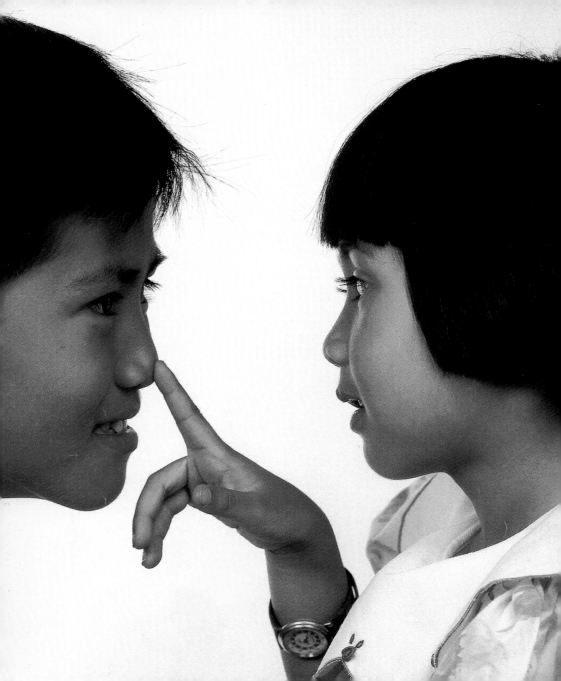

What does Nari touch?

(nose)

Words I Can Read

Nouns

A noun is a person, place, or thing

fun (FUHN) p. 5
horse (HORSS) p. 15
inner tube (IN-ur TOOB) p. 13
kitten (KIT-uhn) p. 17
lawn (LAWN) p. 11
net (NET) p. 7
nose (NOHZ) p. 21
tire (TIRE) p. 9

Proper Nouns

A proper noun is the name
of a person, place, or thing

Nami (NOM-ee) p. 19
Nari (NAR-ee) p. 21
Nat (NAT) p. 15
Nate (NATE) p. 13
Ned (NED) p. 5

Verbs

A verb is an action or being word

More Nn Words

neck

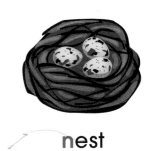

nest

nickel

nine

24